WHERE TIGERS WOULD FEAR TO TREAD

WHERE TIGERS WOULD FEAR TO TREAD

An irreverent, incredible and
slightly insane look at golf's past, present and future

Graham Pilsworth

KEY PORTER BOOKS

National Library of Canada Cataloguing in Publication Data

Pilsworth, Graham, 1944–
    Where tigers would fear to tread

ISBN 1-55263-350-0

1. Golf – Caricatures and cartoons. 2. Canadian wit and humor, Pictorial. I. Title.

NC1449.P62A4 2001   741.5′971   C2001-930788-8

CANADA COUNCIL | LE CONSEIL DES ARTS
FOR THE ARTS | DU CANADA
SINCE 1957 | DEPUIS 1957

The publisher gratefully acknowledges the support of the Canada Council for the Arts and the Ontario Arts Council for its publishing program.

We acknowledge the financial support of the Government of Canada through the Book Publishing Industry Development Program (BPIDP) for our publishing activities.

Key Porter Books Limited
70 The Esplanade
Toronto, Ontario
Canada M5E 1R2

www.keyporter.com

Design: Peter Maher
Electronic formatting: Jean Lightfoot Peters

Printed and bound in Canada

00 01 02 03 04 6 5 4 3 2 1

For Jamie, Caitlin and Nik,
who graciously pussyfooted around while
I was preoccupied with having
a tiger by the tale.

Contents

Introduction

Not long ago, while watching a televised golf tournament, I woke to hear the announcer tallying Tiger Woods' score—287 strokes, I thought I heard, ahead of his nearest rival. I watched as Tiger gave a flex and an arm-pump. He finished his victory flourish with a serene doff of the cap, unleashing a clatter of appreciative applause from the gallery. The entire audience—a sizable number given the golfer on the green—was smiling the type of smile reserved for a warm bath after a grueling day: comforted, content, relaxed. They (and the rest of us) could only marvel at the pantheon level of Tiger's game. It's a wonder he walks and golfs among us.

The media tells us that golf is a game of pure skill, unrivaled in terms of technical precision. It's also breathtakingly simple: knock a ball into a predetermined hole from a specified distance using the fewest number of shots. What could be more ingenuous?

Here's the rub. Underneath that childlike simplicity lurks an unparalleled potential for disaster. Think hazards, weather, acts of God. Consider the notion that every shot possesses an equal dose of Good and Evil. Factor in the Dr. Jekyll and Mr. Hyde that dwell inside every player. Ingenuous? I think not. When all is said and

Dr. Jekyll and Mr. Hyde

done, golf's not a game of how, but how many—about as easy to play as falling up.

What, then, is golf's appeal? What could possibly account for its amazing, ongoing popularity? A quick look at some rival sports tells at least part of the tale. Football, rugby, hockey? If you're upwards of 18, your sport should not include blown knees, floating bone chips or orthoscopic surgery. Tennis? Too much grunting and sweating. Sailing? If you're the skipper, you might as well be back at your desk (unless you find stress relaxing). If you're the crew, that influential weight you think you carry is (face it) ballast.

Golf, on the other hand, has a lot going for it. For one thing, a person can look good while playing. This is important. Everyone—from those so thin that they have to rent shadows to those with 50-inch waists and size 6 shoes—wants to look good. Golf's also got that full seduction arc. It's sensual, energizing, relaxing. Was it good for me? For you? You bet. Golf romances you. It woos you into believing that, in its company, you too will be sleek, sophisticated and sharky.

Never mind that love's always blind. Forget the fact that love lies. Few golfers care. The force of the seduction even supersedes that age-old reality check. In golf, as in life, Murphy's Law states that if anything can possibly go wrong, it will. Dissuasive? Not in

Golf's full seduction arc: sleek, sophisticated and sharky

the least. Nothing dampens the zeal of the bona fide golf nut. In the wonderful world of golf, Murphy's Law seems to exist merely to keep players in line—in line, that is, for instructors, video aids, lucky shirts, hats and instant problem-solver equipment. For struggling tennis players, the latter means racket heads the size of trampolines. For the duffer, it's fat-headed clubs that resemble wheels of cheese, a hedge against that day when clubs and balls with miniaturized missile guidance systems finally become available.

Golf nuts are so in thrall with the game that most with so-so handicaps will overlook:

- The necessity of hollering "MULLIGAN!" instead of "FORE!" when addressing the ball.
- The need to take a provisional at the tee off.
- The likelihood that the only great shot of the day will be served up at the bar.
- The fact that they are playing with clubs autographed by a NASCAR driver who has never set foot on a green.
- The strange quirk of magnetism that (*a*) attracts small rubber-compound spheroids to sand and water, and (*b*) contrarily repels them from closely shorn grassy areas.
- The need to label whimpering, growling, hissing and signs of depression (loss of appetite, panting, rapid heart rate, restless-ness, drooling and dilated pupils) as excuses for a backswing with the putter.
- The propensity that others in the foursome have to whistle the "Colonel Bogey March" between shots.

Paganica?

To these poor souls, an identification with the pro game matters not at all. The machine like precision of Tiger will elude most duffers in perpetuity. And the stately lawns of the pro circuit are not for them. For most, the chance of playing on those hallowed greens lurks somewhere between zero and none. At a glance, duffers and pros play the same game with the same rules. But the buck stops there. Today, golf exists as two almost distinct entities—the rawboned, "fire-in-the-hole" throwback to the mythical Highland version and the pro game's courtly dance.

Recently, while perusing a historical tome, my attention was arrested by a jarring item. It seems that, prior to the advent of the sport that we know as golf, the ancient Romans played *paganica*. By all accounts, paganica was a golf-like game that had players using a wooden club with a curved tip to whack a leather ball stuffed with flock (ends of wool carding, I'm told).

I could well imagine the Roman history of a game with the word "pagan" in it—and how that game would have been co-opted by a society with an insatiable hunger for vicious spectacle.

Picture the Colosseum, a scene of intense excitement. As the blood-thirsty imperator Nero looks on, the paganics *parade about the field. They stop opposite the imperator's box and offer a traditional salute:* "Ave, Nero, no morituri te salutamus!" *("Hail, Nero, we who are about to die wish you health!")*

The paganics gathered on this scorching day are professionals. There are others—from private club members to skilled amateurs and lowly duffers—but this match is not for them. They should thank their lucky stars. In theory, a victorious paganic could become a wealthy public idol; but few are lucky enough to savor their just rewards. Under Nero's watchful eye, paganica is a dangerous game. Often, wild animals appear mid-match—raised on lifts from cages below to insert an element of tooth and claw. A watery motif is another of the imperator's favorites, achieved by flooding the arena to allow seafaring pirates access to the match.

Could this be right? Was this really the start of this hallowed game we call golf?

PART ONE

The Past

History is:
A lie [golf?] agreed upon.
—Anon (abridged)

Fables by the winners.
—Mordant Mary

1

Following the Links
How golf got from there to here

This is how I imagine golf's beginnings. On the sidehill of a wind-blasted crag in the Scottish moors—where the words "harsh" and "severe" describe August—stand a pair of shepherds. Heavy kilts flattened against their massive thighs, these human Clydesdales pass the time by using gnarled sticks to chip small stones into hoofprint divots left by their highland flock. Above them, dense, slate-gray clouds stampede across a leaden sky. One shepherd thrusts his stick skyward and bellows to his companion: "Lay on, Macduffer, and damn'd be he that first cries 'Mulligan!'"

Oh, aye. Ach, no. Absolutely MacWrongo. History books beg to differ. Switch the scene, please, to Holland. Oh, aye. And thank you.

Holland? I couldn't get my mind around this. It would be easier to believe that the tango originated in a yurt on the grasslands of Outer Mongolia. But the historians have spoken. Holland it is. Golf's first year? Try 1296.

The Follies of 1296

Very, very successful years usually toss up one or two benchmark events. Think 1928—penicillin. How do you locate a benchmark event? The quickest, easiest method is to list those events that nobody (apart from historians) has ever heard of and then eliminate them. What's left is the benchmark. Usually.

Noteworthy events tend to be important—political turning points, advancements in science, disasters of all shapes, sizes and persuasions. For our intents and purposes, however, only one criterion needs to be met: Did the event add to our fun quotient? Let's consider this question as it relates to some of 1296's more notable events.

- John de Baliol resigns the Scottish throne (an indented rock that acted triply as throne, grain-pestle and primitive sitz bath) to Edward the First. The throne moves from Scone to Westminster.
- *The Harrowing of Hell*, an early English miracle play, is written. A lutenist options it for a musical, retitles it *The Follies of 1296*, and loses his jerkin.
- Under the direction of Arnolfo di Cambio, crews begin building the Cathedral of Florence. Not to be outdone, fair Florence's miserly sister commissions the Basilica of Lucretia, but (once the estimates come in) settles for a small unnamed shrine.
- Back from the court of Kublai Khan, Marco Polo languishes in a Genoese jail, dictating his memoirs. In them, he describes for

the first time (in a language other than Chinese) such substances as gunpowder and spaghetti.

- In the Andes, South Americans build cable bridges across deep canyons, initiating the first llama traffic tie-ups on the spans.
- Eyeglasses become common. So does divorce. A woman, a first-time eyeglass wearer, is shocked to see that she has been married to a laundry hamper for the past ten years.
- Pope Boniface, presaging insult comedians and badly behaved athletes, entertains himself by kicking an envoy in the face and throwing ashes in the eyes of an archbishop. The painter Giotto mysteriously advances art by getting along with Pope Boniface. The secret? Painting oils of Pope Boniface as a saint.
- Knightwear advances from chain mail to shaped and jointed plate armor. Pleats are optional.
- In the Dutch village of Loenen aan de Vecht, townsfolk invent a game they call *Spel meten Kolven*—which a visiting Spaniard jauntily translates as "put a stave in a wooden shoe and, with it, whack a bound ball of boiled feathers or horsehair all about the town." Those closer to the language translate "Spel" as "to play" and "meten" as "to judge" or "to measure." As for "Kolven," the word elicits giggles and hands pressed to the lips. Ladies and gentlemen, we have our benchmark!

Spel meten Kolven has an auspicious start. From 1296 right up to the end of the seventeenth century, the game spreads like spilled mercury to more than forty townships. Hurriedly passed edicts ban enthusiastic Kolvenists from playing within the city limits. Anyone

Spel meten Kolven—benchmark!

apprehended kolvening in the streets is forced to forfeit his clothes and streak home (surely the world's first skins game).

Then, abruptly, the hoopla is over. Spel meten Kolven disappears. In its place arises *kolf*. An ancient version of mini-golf, kolf is played on shortened courses, thus avoiding the North Rhine roughs in neighboring Germany. Some of these courses are even more drastically truncated when the game moves indoors. Eventually, this early form of pitch and putt also loses its popularity—despite ardent cheerleading and encouragement from those in the window and furniture repair trade. The decline continues until 1890, when the Scottish version of kolf—golf—arrives at The Hague.

The Scottish Connection

To link the Scottish with the Dutch—or golf with kolf—it's necessary to move forward from those halcyon Spel meten Kolven days to a period of close trade ties between Holland and Scotland. During the fifteenth and sixteenth centuries, a Dutch navigational preference for east coast Scottish ports ensures that kolf appears there first. The west Scots simply have to wait. In the meantime, they amuse themselves with games of internecine skirmishing— battling English invaders and transforming haggis from a catapult munition to an edible foodstuff (a miracle of alchemy that continues to elude them).

The earliest reference to Scottish golf appears in King James the Second's decree outrightly banning the game. Ol' Fiery Face (as he is affectionately known to his friends) worries (with some

Ol' Fiery Face drills the troops

justification) that golf's thrall is turning Scots away from
compulsory archery practice. In his mind, at least, there is no
military advantage in fielding an army of sportsmen brandishing
wooden golf clubs. The hated English invaders and their wretched
culinary practices would simply have run amok.

Thankfully, in 1502, the Royal Killjoy attitude succumbs to
the full-serving enthusiasm of a true golf addict: King James the
"Foreth." During his reign, everyone plays—from royals and shepherds to all postings and positions in between. Any suitable tract
of common land is commandeered. Holes are cut in and bunkers
scraped out by sheep sheltering from the ferocious summer breezes.
The equipment? Wooden clubs and wooden balls: clubs go for
a penny apiece, balls for about four pence per dozen. At these
prices, golf is an everyman's game. Too good to be true—or to last.

In 1618, exclusivity rears its elitist head—which, coincidentally,
looks very much like a feather ball, or featherie. The featherie
(boiled feathers wrapped in cowhide) improves the game, despite
flying like a hurled balloon when wet. For the everyman class of
duffers, the problem is cost. As a pastime to take mind and body
away from the harsh and severe, golf is now out of reach for all
but the wealthy. And along with the money come the wash-and-
dressing-up refinements—the beginning of the end of golf's rough
Rob Roy edges.

A case in point: Leith, 1744. Courtesy of Edinburgh, the Leith
links hold a golfing competition, offering up a silver club to the
winner. The tourney is born. As commoners look on (offering up
resentment), the match takes place. Five holes—all set at distances

Founding member: Honorable Company of Edinburgh Golfers (and Freemasons)

of four and five hundred yards—and three circuits comprise a round. The course difficulty (landscaping by North Sea Weather Bombs) is such that competitors are inwardly ecstatic if they manage to get down a hole in five strokes (not weeks).

Twenty years later, the Honorable Company of Edinburgh Golfers (and Freemasons) form the first golf club. Indeed, the Freemasons establish Britain's first golfing societies; the secret handshakes give birth to prototypes of overlapping golf club grips. At the new clubs, w(h)ining and dining are the raison d'être. Golf itself is tolerated as a pre-nosh exercise. It is during this era that The Royal and Ancient Golf Club of St. Andrews is founded. Now the illustrious prefix can be affixed to the word "game."

Elitism continues to grow like paunch on a glutton. The day before a match, club members in elaborate uniforms turn up at a local tavern to scarf down prodigious amounts of food and drink, and arrange motivational wagers on the upcoming round. Not to be outdone by the folk in Leith, members of Prestwick's prestigious club offer a striking red Moroccan leather Challenge Belt, flashily ornamented with silver plates, for their first professional championship.

In 1860, eight players compete with "pro" Willie Park of Musselburgh (home of the Royal Musselburgh Golf Club) on Prestwick's physically daunting twelve-hole course. Park takes the championship with a score of 174 over three circuits. The following

Scots abroad: civilizing the natives

year, the tourney broadens to include amateurs and becomes the first Open Championship.

And then, the big break. In the 1890s, golf is named Scotland's national game. (Haggis hurling is swiftly downgraded to "pastime," while caber tossing is lost to more modern forestry practices.) The game spreads throughout the world as thousands of Scots wrench themselves away from their homeland to teach golf in the farthest regions of the planet, where "harsh" and "severe" are missing from local vocabularies.

New World Order

Golf makes its American premiere during the Revolutionary War, when Scottish officers stationed in Fort Orange, New York, tee off in the face of an ordinance forbidding play of this sort in the streets. The ordinance dates back to the antics of Dutch colonists who tore up the town playing Spel meten Kolven, terrorizing the townsfolk and livestock and shattering windows.

Back in Scotland, there is good news for the dour masses of sidelined Kolvenists. In 1848, someone in Malaya discovers "gutta percha." Initially mistranslated as "filleting a fish," this hard substance is found to be childishly easy to manipulate when softened in water. Tired of shaping gutta percha into puerile novelty jokes, inventive minds turn to rolling the material into balls. Test swatting trials demonstrate that gutta percha balls are too smooth to fly properly. In frustration, a small hammer is taken to a ball,

Hagen wins Brit Open

puckering the surface. When the dimpled ball is tossed aside, it flies wonderfully. Eureka!

The new golf ball—the cheap golf ball—is something of a miracle. Manufacturers swear it will last forever (or at least until the first water hazard). The ball arrives in Scotland to a tumultuous "Hoot, Hoot, Hooray" from the dour Kolvenists. It's the 1880s, and the "gutty" era has dawned. There is, however, a downside. The gutty—so durable, so hard, such a miracle—shatters wooden clubs on impact. Occasionally, the ball itself explodes like a piece of popcorn. Thankfully, the Americans invent a new ball; rubber thread, core-wound. This new miracle flies farther and proves to be easier on clubs. Not surprisingly, it also necessitates longer courses and prompts the evolution of the iron-headed club.

By 1894, golf's popularity is soaring. Having solved the rubber ball dilemma, the Americans turn their attention to bigger fish. Golf, they decide, needs regulating. It's a tall New World Order. Somebody has to do it, so America does. The United States Golf Association is formed and, from this time forward, America dominates the Royal and Ancient game.

In 1904, Walter Travis becomes the first Yank to win the British Amateur Championship—shocking and appalling British golf administrators. Several strongly worded letters are sent to the *Times* in London. In France, there is jubilation.

In the end, Travis' hit will seem like a love tap compared to the punch packed by the first globe-trotting professional—one Walter Hagen. Hagen arrives in England to compete in the 1922 British Open. At that time, the golf pro was still performing his duties "below the stairs," barred from entering the club and mixing with members. In comes Hagen, oblivious to these restrictions. His high-flying lifestyle rocks the gentry, but before more strongly worded letters can be written and sent to the *Times*, the Prince of Wales intervenes. His Royal Highness is absolutely razzle-dazzled by Hagen's charms, and a friendship is struck up. And that means "struck down" for the members, who are forced to slacken their stiff upper lips and lower their social barriers. Hagen rubs it in by winning the British Open, by gad!

Other Americans flex their golfing muscles. Bobby Jones is the

Saint Bobby

first to be offered up for canonization when he completes the Grand Slam—the British Open, the US Open and the Amateur Championship. During Jones' luminous transcendence, the steel shaft gains legitimacy, thus propelling golf into the modern era of equipment.

Enter the Tiger

In 1937, American professionals win Britain's Ryder Cup. In 1968, Arnold Palmer scorches courses and becomes the first player to earn a million dollars in prize winnings. The stage is set for the Golden Bear. In 1975, Jack Nicklaus collects sixteen victories, securing a place in golf history as the most successful professional of his day. Course records fall like pogo-stick jumpers in a room full of ball bearings. The courses themselves become more stylized and manicured; physical embodiments of computer-generated lay-outs—slick, refined, sophisticated.

Enter the Tiger.

PART TWO

The Present

Tyger, Tyger burning bright,
In the forests of the night;
What immortal hand or eye,
Could frame thy fearful symmetry?

—William Blake

2

Tiger Inc.

The greenback greening of golf

For years now, sports fans (zealots excluded) have tended to rank golf somewhere south of the Chevy Nova on the exotic scale. Pros with names like Gary, Arnold, Tom, Johnny and Jack played the PGA Tour with a self-effacing modesty befitting decent Wonder Bread gents. What lay beneath didn't matter. This squeaky-clean image worked—no one felt threatened, and chronic insomniacs were free to click on televised tourneys as the crucial first step in their search for sleep. In September 1996, however, sleeping pill stock rebounded in a big way when young golf upstart Tiger Woods turned pro.

Sleepers and businessmen woke up, sat up and took notice. As Tiger roared and soared, everything changed. Lowly duffers who previously identified with the Golden Bear (his physique, not his game) sat in a stunned stupor, staring in wonder at the svelte specter of this phenom; the latest to descend from that select pantheon of gods whose names become synonymous with their respective sports—Gretzky, Jordan, Ali. Golf had gotten its stripes.

The PGA and business went cha-ching. Here was a young black

urbanite in possession of oodles of charisma, and athletic skill sets ahead by a length of miraculous. Big Money Interests knew a guaranteed one-way bet when they saw one. With Gretzky, Jordan and Ali retired, Big Money had been craving a new superstar. Now they had one, and the relentless greenback greening of the greens began. The mid-level success of the golf business jumped to heights unimaginable BT—Before Tiger. Riding Big Money's booster rocket, the PGA lifted off and the Tiger swooshed.

It was a breathtaking transformation. Once a charming pastime—where the successful knocking about of a featherie on a hardscrabble course could earn one a snazzy championship belt—golf suddenly had hundreds of millions at stake. What started as a game had become a Mega Business. Hardcore fans pored over tournament scores as avidly as they ogled the stock market crawls—it helped to have an MBA. (Lest we forget, there are still heretics who golf for fun; and others who mix their fun with business. More on these special interest groups later.)

If golf has truly become a Mega Business—and who can doubt that it has—then Tiger Woods is its front man. Without too much imagination, it's possible to think of him not as a person, but as a corporate entity. Call it Tiger Inc. As with most businesses, this one has its controlling interests. By consulting this helpful pie chart, we can see that those with a stake in Tiger

Tiger Inc.

Inc.'s success are the PGA, television, equipment and clothing manufacturers and course developers and architects.

But First, a Word from Our Sponsors

Let's make one thing clear: not every golfer gets to be a business
in and of himself. Certain criteria must be met. Certain standards
must be upheld. Not everyone is cut out for the job. Tiger Woods is.

Not only can Tiger swing a golf club, he can swing one heck
of a clothing deal. Try on $100,000,000 over five years. Nice fit?
The clothing sure makes this man. Cutting such deals cuts to the
heart of golf's status as a Mega Business. This search for parity with
the National Treasury (or Bill Gates) has become the pro golfer's
Holy Grail.

As with most quests, this one's easier imagined than achieved.
To even rate a look-in from most sponsors, a golfer must become a
household name. Dust Bunny should be ruled out: it's bad enough
to be a rabbit on the tour. Aspiring Tigers everywhere should note
the following three requirements.

- *Physique*: It's de rigueur to flaunt the highly trained body of an
  Olympic high-diver (not the paunch from training high in an
  Olympic dive).
- *Cutes*: Warm eyes (brown, Bambi-like), shy smile and soft, even
  features. If the words "vulpine," "cadaverous" or "Quasimodo-
  like" apply to you, you've got trouble.

- *Great nickname*: You have little hope for success with a nom de guerre like Weasel, Goofball or Slicin'.

If you somehow manage to meet these criteria, you've got a shot. But are you the right caliber? Success can be as difficult to handle as the lack thereof. Is success worth the effort expended to achieve it? All those hours lying there dreaming—is there a positive payoff in the end? Consider this. Very successful people like Tiger Woods are apt to become jaded and look for new and higher marks of success. If money's no objective in your game, what's left? The penultimate? A demigod or idol to millions? Intentionally or not, Tiger's on this path. How to tell?

- Fans want to rub his mashie for luck and/or to cure the yips.
- CEO golf zealots insist on sacrificing fattened calves (in the form of preferred stock options) in his name.
- Vestal virgins, otherwise known as Babes in the Woods, follow him everywhere.
- His divots are said to miraculously self-heal.
- Men, apart from Tiger, are deemed redundant. From this point on, the male gender will be supplied by Tiger cloning.

Be warned. There is a drawback to becoming an idol. Religious

Vestal virgins

fanatics may blow you up as a graven image. Still keen? Fame, that temptress or tempter, throws off a beguiling odor—the sweet smell of success. As Tiger Woods exudes this heady bouquet like a vapor trail from an ascending rocket, it's worthwhile for aspiring Tigers to study him for helpful tips.

Becoming a Tiger won't be easy. Make no bones about it: advice can be offered, but (and there's always a but) the sad fact is "ya gotta dance with the genes what brung ya." If you're closer, genetically speaking, to goats or sloths, it's unlikely you'll make it as a Tiger. So there you are. But then again, if no one had dreams, there'd be no psychoanalysts—or Craig Stadler. He had some fine moments in the sun as the Walrus, "goo goo goo joob." Hope springs eternal.

HELPFUL TIPS FOR ASPIRING TIGERS

- Change your surname to a golf club moniker. Tiger has Woods. You can claim Irons. Less favorable for endorsement name-branding potential? Wedge, Mashie, Niblick.
- When it comes to corporate sponsorship, think big league. Local car dealerships, pizza outlets and electrical and plumbing suppliers are best left to slo-pitch leagues. Be wary of endorsing non-golf products. Lawn-care treatments are acceptable; Forest Lawn–care is not.
- Never base caddy selection on phrenology.
- If a prospective agent/manager exhibits any or all of these three P-words—phlegmatic, piratical, pariah—just say no, or move on to a more advantageous letter of the alphabet.

The PGA: Golf's Big Show

Every sport has its professional level, usually referred to as The Bigs or The Big Show. For golf, The Big Show is the PGA—which exists primarily as Tiger Inc.'s game preserve.

Up until Tiger's ascent to The Big Show, the PGA spluttered along as a somewhat obscure cottage industry. On television, it was a twelve-second stop on the way to NASCAR or the football game. One can confidently speculate that without Tiger Woods, golf would still be mired in *Caddyshack* imagery and draped in banlon. (Anyone troubled by the roil of big money churning up the game should keep banlon in mind when spurred to grouse.)

In their largesse as a team, Tiger and the PGA dictate golf's mores. And that cuts to Big Golf's core value; namely, what's good for golf is good for corporate America. By extension, it's also good for you—the golfer, the fan, the consumer. In a nutshell, PGA golf likens itself to the apogee of human existence. Without golf, life would not be worth living. It's a little thing, but it means a lot.

Because of this highly self-important role, the PGA must be very circumspect when it comes to their spokespeople and superstars. Take Tiger for instance. Why does he perfectly fit the bill?

TEN THINGS TIGER IS NOT
1. An annoying walking billboard and in-your-face pitchman for Adidas, Adidas, Adidas.
2. Hockey player "Gums" Hooligan, trying to smart off in recognizable sentence structure.

3. *Biography* fodder for "Bandito" Pete: The Wastrel Tennis Years.
4. Linebacker 'Roids Rager, stomping opponents with his cleats to impress Jodie Foster.
5. A chewin', tobacco juice spittin', lug nut adjustin' baseball doofus.
6. The San Diego Chicken.
7. Feature material for *Architectural Digest*'s look at revamping the Winnebago.
8. Golfshoe Gomer, hawking Double-knit Mix and Matchables.
9. Fuzzy Zoeller.
10. A heartbeat away from the presidency of the United States of America.

Tiger's vast success and wide exposure mean a great deal to many, many organizations. For the PGA, Tiger means:

- No longer being mistaken for the Poughkeepsie Garment-workers Association—the other PGA.
- No more waterslide parks for the kiddies and faked-up Elvis sightings to entertain adults.
- No more snide comparisons: e.g., golf is to excitement what Gregorian chants are to the bluegrass banjo.
- No more fans saying: "This sucks, let's go indoor go-carting."
- No more having to show three pieces of ID and a list of legitimate references before fielding a lineup of players for the Masters.

There are other benefits, as well. "Dowdy" and "dull" have become high-concept action terms. PGA officials now routinely wear weightlifting belts when carrying their wallets. Painted crowd backdrops and mannequin galleries have finally been replaced by real fans. And...drum roll please...after years of languishing in near obscurity, golf has finally overtaken billiards in the quest for World Sports Supremacy.

In Big Show terms, only satire closes Saturday night. As Big Shows go, Tiger Inc./PGA is *Masterpiece Theater* jumped up for fans, scratch players, scramblers, hackers and the duffers of St. Petersburg's stately lawns. Barring a tragic hang-glider mishap in Nepal, Tiger promises a very long run with no closing in sight. The show? *(Tiger) Cats.*

A Picture Is Worth a Thousand Sales

Business reports on wild stock market swings and TV newscasts have a number of distasteful side effects: frayed nerves, unsightly stains, the yips. It's safe to say that the current imbroglios in world and business affairs are tugging people back to a state of mind one might accurately describe as lily-dipping. Less frenetic; more relaxed. For Big Golf, this is terrific news.

If you think de-stressing is leaving the cell phone at home, palming off the Palm Pilot or making the switch from fast food to leisure, you'd be wrong. For a good many of us, the chosen method of blissing out has absolutely nothing to do with saying "no" to the

Know your audience: football versus golf

apparatuses of commerce, and everything to do with embracing the fantasyland of televised sports.

But does this really offer relief? Not usually. Jangling commercials fill the beginning, middle and end of each program, turning television into electric ire. And with sponsors calling the tune, what are the poor networks to do? If they didn't fill twenty-nine minutes out of every thirty with advertisements, there'd be a major crimp in sports offerings. Broadcasters would be forced to show grainy images of tractor pulls packaged by those sporting cutups at Vladivostock TV, sponsored in part by feed lot suppliers. Aargh!

Of all the prodigiously popular sports, only Tiger Inc. represents a happy alternative. Gone is the incessant hyperactive auctioneer delivery style, with its intrusive off-the-meds computer graphics popping up on screens like firework warm-ups for the next millennium celebration. Golf broadcasters know their audiences, and they know the magnetism of their ace-in-the-hole. It's happy days for Big Golf's balance sheets as fans old and new are drawn—in ever increasing numbers—to watch the cool cat at work.

Why do they watch? The reasons are many and varied.

- Allergies, not golf, ruin a good walk. This way, the eyes don't get puffy from natural causes.
- What better way to find out what happened to Ernie Els?
- Rearranging the kitchen junk drawer just doesn't cut it for edge-of-your-seat, spine-tingling excitement.
- It's a great way to see what hottie colors go with green.
- It's still the best way to doze off uninterrupted since the invention of the wee small hours of the morning.

How is this rarified atmosphere achieved? It's all in the broadcasting.

TEN TIPS FOR SUCCESSFUL GOLF BROADCASTING

1. Employ measured tones befitting a game of skill and precision—or a state funeral.
2. Have the ability to describe an entire tournament in five hundred words or less.
3. Be able to resist fooling around by scrambling the word order of sentences like "this for birdie on eleven."

4. Refrain from rumor mongering about road rage on the driving range.

5. Have great bladder control. It's one afternoon, thirty cups of coffee and one pair of pants in the broadcast truck.

6. Curb acerbic asides: e.g., "In the time it takes to line up this putt, we could whip up an exotic fruit flan from scratch."

7. Never suggest that golf could be spiced up if the rules were relaxed to permit chest bumps, head butts and forearm bangs with caddies.

8. Never attempt to describe action taking place below the threshold of normal awareness.

9. Know that silence is golden, but not worth listening to the broadcaster's pulse.

10. Remember that, while it's doubtlessly true that people love colorful commentary, they tend to balk at the use of language like: "It's been a holy war from the first tee"; "There's a shooting standoff on seven"; or "Lock an' load, baby, lock an' load."

As everyone who has ever watched televised golf knows, it's 95 percent golf and 5 percent talk. Is silence golden? It is to the advertisers. TV golf advertising is no billion-dollar yawn treatment. There's simply less yodeling to distract the viewer from what's really important—the logo placements. The strategy is sound. As burgeoning sales attest, this is a medium well done.

Endorsements Make the World Go Around

Looking at Tiger Woods, what words spring to mind? Elegance?
Class? Cool? It's more than obvious that this athlete is not sporting
a look fashioned by The Whammo Company. Put it this way: Tiger
Woods is the Fred Astaire of golf. Watch him address the ball.
Notice the languid upswing; the pause at the top. Catch the
manufacturer's logo on the driver? Of course you did. He gave
you time. Now the downswing, 125 miles per hour. Did you hear
it go swoosh? That's the idea. Then, the perfect follow-through
into the classic finishing pose. See the Nike symbol on the hat?
How could you not? You gotta love—if you're an advertiser.

Businessmen know full well that it takes more than great
technique to make an outstanding golfer. There are clothes and
equipment at work, too. And both the golfer and the business
profit from that work. Handsomely. Sharply. With the support
of their wares, the golfer need only to win games and pile up
the glory. After a few moments in a new outfit, armed with
new hi-tech styled clubs, even those with two-figure handicaps
are suddenly reborn—liberated to overcome inhibitions and unlock
hidden talents.

Can these claims really be so? They sound almost too good to
be true. Look around, say the manufacturers. Compare those who
embrace the new with those who don't. Take careful notice that
the golfers sporting splendid games are happy, rich and very well
turned-out with the latest equipment and outfits. Note that those
struggling with their game are unhappy, forced to get by on good

Men's golf garb—then and now

connections and hard work. They doggedly cling to outdated equipment and clothes, relying instead on skill, stamina and the courage of Lassie for their just rewards on the links. Gives one pause....

How, then, does one halt game retrogression and decline when money is an object? New equipment can be expensive. More lessons? More clinics? Sadly, all the clinics and the lessons in the world will not compensate for inferior equipment. You are not impressing anyone with the bold simplicity of clubs once new in 1953. And clothing? It shouldn't beg the question, "Are you that concerned about your dependents?"

Understand this. To perfect a highly effective golf game, the player, clubs and ball must blend like the instruments in a symphony orchestra. To achieve this, each instrument, when isolated, must be seen as a complex factor in and of itself, deserving serious individual attention. Why? It's the variables in good equipment that make the difference between skill and skulling. These include lie, flex, material and lengths of shafts, grip size, swing weight, loft, face angle and club head design. And all of these relate to the "whole" in one.

This is all well and good, but there's a nagging sense that, despite all the manufacturers' blandishments that their club and your hands combine to make the world's best weapon against shanks, slices and hooks, it ain't necessarily so. It could be just as viable to say a better class of club in your hands means you get to accidentally coldcock a better class of opponent. But don't despair. Study the illustrations of then (at the beginning of golf's modern age) and now; they'll do wonders for your self-esteem. And remember, whether it's clothing or equipment, fashion goes in one year and out the other.

If You Build It, They Will Come

Television loves to flash the immediacy card. Without a soupçon of self-effacement, it likes to claim that it—and only it—puts you, the viewing public, smack dab in the thick of things. That's *you* trading barbs with world leaders, dodging bullets in warring hot spots or rubbing shoulders at the Masters. Be there, TV exhorts, with Tiger, Jack and Vijay.

Women's golf garb—then and now

But for pro golf, this would be a moot point (mute, for the advertisers) if the actual playing facilities were not there. If a developer's eye hadn't seen the potential for a world-class golf course on a lot just off Magnolia Lane, next to the Augusta Country Club, then Augusta National would never have been Mastered. Big Golf might have consisted of a troop of cigar-chomping guys in loud suits barnstorming the nation hawking parlor pitch and putt sets. Tiger Woods might have been a big cat enclave in India. The mind boggles.

It will come as a great surprise to absolutely no one that golf course development is not a quick and easy way to profit. The task is labyrinthine in scope and complexity.

Of Sharks and Dreamers

There you are, a zealous golfer with lots on the mind; lots of land, that is. You've been standing for hours—with your clubs and a two-day change of clothes—in a queue at your local links, waiting for a tee off time. To pass the hours, you dream about building your own course. In the fantasy, it's a one-two-three proposition. One: find a parcel of suitable land. Two: seize her. Three: Augusta! So, you think, how hard can this be? Instructions for operating a ball washer are more complicated. The concept appears innocent enough—get land, create business plan, obtain building permit, hire a golf architect/course designer, secure financing, dream up a suitable name.

The last could be the trickiest part. Whether you're based in Moose Jaw, Hoboken or Saint Moritz, it's currently de rigueur to give your course a Spanish name. It's romantic, and, like loose-fitting clothes, it can cover a host of physical imperfections. Costa de la Luz. Palmas Del Mar. Cabo del Sol. These are bona fide course names. What's in a name? Just this. Your links is in Moose Jaw, Saskatchewan, Canada. It's late July. Snow's up to your peduncles. You need people to come and enrich you with daily fees. So, what's more attractive? White Christmas in July Golf and Country Club, or Qué Tiemp Más Feo? I rest my case. (It translates roughly as What Awful Weather, in case you were wondering.)

Back to the issue at hand. Developers in the know would put you, the neophyte, into one of four golf course developer categories.

- *The Sharks*: Corporations who never build anything. They simply circle the Dreamers and bide time as construction begins. When the bleeding starts, the Sharks move in to chow down cheap.
- *The Mayors*: Builders that play by winter rules with their municipalities' public money. Mayors use golf courses to improve the quality of municipal life for those they refer to in sentences that begin, "My friends...."
- *The Millionaires*: Deep-pocket people in the game for two reasons—fun and a munificent legacy. Course membership is

Dinner, anyone?

restricted to those with medical specialist degrees or a high-net-worth Fortune 500 ranking.

- *The Dreamers*: Incurable golf romantics with vast enthusiasm and slender means. Their quixotic mission to create a feast of greens for all usually comes acropper and ends up a tossed green salad for Sharks.

Someone once called dreams the pauper's movie. This is close to the mark. Those lush lawns you dream about could just as easily become the bottomless quagmire of nightmares. Consider:

Land. Big problems here with purchasing and obtaining permits. You could be in trouble eyeing:

- An ancient battlefield site held in trust by local historical societies until such time as a reasonable counteroffer to yours comes in from Wal-Mart's people;
- An Indian burial ground and/or future casino site;
- Land zoned as agricultural; no, wait, housing with some agricultural usage; no, wait, conservation parkland with no agricultural usage but some housing; no, wait, some housing but no conservational applications; no, wait....

Course architect/designer. With your limited funds, you could be saddled with:

- A designer whose landscaping plan contains the expression "scorched earth";

- A designer who proclaims the overall color motif as mauve, sees the greens in shag carpeting and the bunkers full of Wiffle balls;
- A designer whose previous landscaping job involved a rake and a jumbo orange leaf bag.

Financing. Consider the venture capitalization differences between you and the Millionaires.

- Millionaires have bankers as best friends. For you, bankers are paramedics with lousy bedside manners;
- Millionaires have launches with prospective investors. You're lucky to have lunches;
- Millionaires' proposals put prime farmland to a far nobler use; yours upgrades a toxic landfill dump to a blot on the landscape.

For big-time developers, the golf course is merely a loss-leader for the real money—condos and resort complexes. Dreamers hoping to make money from golf course development should just forget it. It's as easy as matching plaids. So, if you're shuffling your feet in that long queue—waiting for a tee off time before your next birthday and musing about building your own golf home on the range—keep this question in mind: What kind of hen lays the longest? (Answer: A dead one.)

Caddyshack Buffs Need Not Apply

Among the welter of ancillary golf vocations, none is more aesthetically compelling than architecture. What could be more soul stirring (aside from being the first amateur to win the Grand Slam) than acquiring riches and fame by designing landscapes that correct Nature's vulgarity?

A geographic axiom states that the planet Earth is 75 percent water. That leaves available 25 percent of the planet's surface above sea level for the practice of golf course architecture and design. That golf architects must share the space with lesser interests (vibrant cities, prosperous farming enterprises, parkettes, theme parks) is, in their estimation, an unacceptable encroachment. They believe that golf links the world.

To be tops in this vocation, a course designer should possess a number of skills—knowledge of the game, training, experience enough to turn out a course deemed both playable and aesthetically appealing. The designer must be able to switch from eye visor to hard hat in order to manage his or her vision as it's being constructed.

When all is said and done, the designer's most valuable asset might be a multipronged hat rack with spaces for a minimum of nine hats.

THE COURSE DESIGNER'S NINE HATS

1. *A golf hat.* The architect must have an intimate working knowledge of each aspect of the game. Memorized dialogue from the movie *Caddyshack* is considered a negative factor.
2. *A civil engineer's cap.* The architect must demonstrate an ability to read and use contour maps to ensure proper topographical plans that include cut and fill, drainage and course routes. Golfers would be singularly unamused if subjected to

"You've got to be joking."

playing in a hedgerow maze, a topiary garden or a park of leaning obelisks.

3. *A hydraulic engineering cap.* The architect must have a working knowledge of pumping stations and the techie wherewithal to design manual and automatic irrigation systems. A golfer should not be forced to tread water at tee off, buck a surging fairway current or worry about bog conditions on the greens.

4. *A landscape architecture hat.* The architect must have the sensitivity and aesthetic wit to work with nature. An understanding of preservation and soil preparation is a given. Golfers

generally frown upon flora landscaping from the nurseries of Worldwide Plastics.

5. *An agronomist's cap.* The architect must have a thorough understanding of soil fertility and drainage to ensure the proper selection of grass. The golfer must be relaxed in the knowledge that the designer has properly laid turfgrass and not, say, elephant grass with blades that could shatter a lawnmower.

6. *A soil chemist's hat.* The architect's knowledge base must include the skinny on fertilizers, fungicides and weed-killers. The golfer must not feel that he's playing the Toxic Chemical Golf and Country Club, that the fairway grass has developed a belligerent personality or that the back nine has the nitrate volatility of a mine field.

7. *A surveyor's cap.* The architect should come prepared and equipped to operate an engineer's transit for staking and checking grades. Golfers are known to complain if they find it necessary to employ Sherpa guides, gondoliers or subway inspectors as caddies.

8. *A heavy-construction hat.* The architect must oversee the operations of clearing, grubbing, earthmoving, drainage, irrigation installation and planting preparation. It is thus necessary to have a detailed knowledge of light and heavy construction machinery to ensure completion of a course truly representational of the standard traditions of golf. Needless to say, a golfer would balk at playing a course resembling The Daytona 500 Speedway, the Bonneville Salt Flats or the Hope Slide.

9. *A cost estimator's hat.* It's very important that the architect have

the budgeting skills to itemize costs so that appropriate funding can be secured. How disappointed the golfer would be teeing off to play eighteen on a course the size of a toupee.

Golf course architects are not practitioners of the superfluous. They like to be thought of as counterbalances to a gluttonous diet of steel, concrete, glass and chrome. After all, a diet is hardly balanced without its greens.

Bonneville Salt Flats Golf and Country Club

3

Sealing the Deal

How to succeed in golf without really trying

There are some things that have natural affinities: lettuce and mayo, treasure and island, peptic and ulcer. So it is with business and golf. This is one merger made in heaven. Never mind that golf—with its relaxed pace and peaceful settings—offers a perfect place for the touchy-feely, get-to-know-you kind of business that's currently all the rage. Golf and business have a much deeper history. Even their terminologies have a synchronicity. We'll reference *Davies' Dictionary of Golfing Terms* and compare.

A merger made in heaven

Pitch. *In golf:* To play (the ball) in a steep trajectory, typically with considerable backspin; usually as an approach shot or over difficulty. *In business*: To sell a play (the product or stock option) with ascending hyperbole, typically with considerable spin (top or under); usually as an approach shot (regular buyer) or over difficulty (cold call).

Chip. *In golf*: A short, moderately lofted approach shot with little backspin. *In business*: High-priced stocks (better known as blue chips) with moderately rising earnings with little or no backspin (stability).

Drive. *In golf*: To hit (the ball or a shot) with a full stroke, generally using one's maximum power; to play such a shot from the tee, especially using a driver. *In business*: To relentlessly and powerfully move fast from a starting point, usually trying to avoid a full stroke.

Tee off. *In golf*: To play a tee shot; to play a shot from a teeing ground. *In business*: To verbally attack somebody with great vigor, anger and disgust. (Not to be confused with an *eff* off, which often coincides with a tee off from a teeing off ground.)

Ball. *In golf*: The hard and resilient spheroid projectile used to play. Usually of solid compressed synthetic rubber, colored white and with several hundred indentations on the surface. *In business*: Usually plural; the hard and resilient spheroids used in risky business plays. Often made of solid, compressed brass.

Club. *In golf:* Any of the various implements used to strike the ball. *In business:* Any of the various exclusive establishments used in business to cement the deal.

Iron. *In golf:* A club with a head made of iron or (in modern times) steel. *In business:* An inflexible person with a head made of iron or (in modern times) bone.

Scorecard. *In golf:* A card on which scores are recorded in stroke play. *In business:* A quarterly earnings report. During downturns, scores are sometimes recorded while having strokes.

Spot the dealmakers

Par. *In golf*: The standard score, in strokes, assigned to each hole of a course. Assigned on the basis of one, two or three strokes through the green to the length of the hole, plus two putts. Represents the standard of play expected of a first-class player in favorable conditions making no mistakes. *In business*: The average or normal level of unassisted anxiety, stress and exhilaration in a place of business, as in "this is par for the course today." Also refers to dealmaking based on the value of metal in each party's spine.

The fit? Hand in golf glove. Quid pro quo.

The stickiest issue confronting those who combine golf with business is business golf's specialized code of behavior and etiquette. After determining whether you are the party being worked or the party working, you must devise a workable game plan to ensure the desired par for the course: a sweet deal.

Survival of the Fittest?

A military campaign style of strategizing is counterproductive for securing links. With its take-no-prisoners, law-of-the-jungle and lone-gunman-of-the-Wild-West undertones, this approach stands out as a win-lose scenario (you win, your business loses). Instead, take a provisional (or a Valium) and think like Darwin.

Most people equate Darwin with making a monkey out of man—and there's very little room for argument when one compares chimps to chumps. But the golf course is naturally not the

Galapagos. If it were, we could devise a workable strategy based on evolution's pattern for survival—namely, adapt and adopt. Adapt your game to the conditions and adopt a strategy to ensure a win-win situation for both you and the party you're working.

This strategy only works if you have a firm grasp of your subject. Play could be affected by incorrect information and erroneous assumptions. Consider a sense of humor, for example. You assume he's got one. You're wrong. The results could be disastrous, or spectacular, depending on your goal.

TEN WAYS TO UNNERVE THE HUMORLESS WONDER

1. Announce that you learned everything you know about golf from the "Book of Revelations."

2. Remark that the position he assumes while putting has been known to cause impotency.

3. Observe that he swings like Tiny Tim and putts like King Kong.

4. Admit that you haven't seen divots that size since a backhoe dug a sewer trench through your backyard.

5. Ask permission to lift and drop your ball without penalty under the relief rule. Base this request on casual water interference caused by his nervous sweat.

The return of King Kong

6. Wonder aloud if her misreading of the greens suggests a failing grade in golf literacy.
7. Ask if his explosion shots have in any way been hampered by international test ban agreements.
8. Speculate that if she had a dollar value attached to every shot she sclaffed she could be sclaffing all the way to the bank.
9. Warn him that his overlapping grip should not include your clubs, too.
10. Glue a marshmallow to the club face of her driver to guarantee hitting the sweet spot.

There's no doubt that a careful sizing up is essential. If you want to be truly successful, it's necessary to feng shui your game's alignment. If you are a Tiger and your subject's a scrambler (or worse, a hacker), you must resign yourself to schluff shot-making. Think of it as pain for gain.

The Fine Art of Schluffing

What exactly is schluffing? Bluntly, it's a technique for losing your excellent shots. Stance plays an imperative role when it comes to the perfect schluff. Some people find this difficult. Golfers do, too. Despite the challenges, the fine art of schluffing has been in practice for time immemorial. History offers many, many examples—Genghis Khan was a schluffer of note; Mary Queen of Scots was another. August company indeed, but schluffing is hardly

Successful schluffing stances

a source of pride. It does, however, come shrouded in mystery and legend. Among the most well-known schluffing myths:

- It causes your skeleton to pretzel.
- It leaves you hanging from trees.
- It lines you up catastrophically with most of the lesser planets.
- It's slimy.

Those who know say it's all worth the risk. A well-timed schluff-putt—no matter how dangerous or deadly—can save a deal. An example will help us illustrate the point. Let's suppose your subject plays a hole as seen in the accompanying chart. As shown, you're on the green in two; your quarry, in five. Three putts and he's finally down, meaning you have to six-putt in order to win-lose the hole.

Now this is where the true beauty of the schluff reveals itself. By keeping four simple things in mind, you'll be able to schluff-putt your way to glory—or at least to a higher tax bracket. The key is a misreading of the green. (If you're scoffing at the mere thought, get over yourself. Misread you must.) Once you achieve this, the four tenets will fall nicely into place. They are:

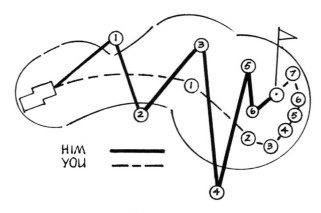

Schluff-play strategy

- Don't drop your putt while practicing your stroke.
- Don't keep your eyes open while putting.
- Don't play the breaks like the ball has eyes when yours are closed.
- Don't play in the heat of the midday sun. If you've got a hot hand on the putter, you can't cool down. Wait until after dusk.

Mastering these basics is merely the tip of the schluffing iceberg. Truly spectacular schluff work can require some fancy foot-in-mouth work. Should your schluffing by some mischance or another raise suspicions that could lower your expectations, you might consider employing one of the following ready-made excuses.

FOUR SCHLUFF-PROOF EXCUSES

1. "On afternoons such as this, I suffer from an undercurrent of minor convulsions caused by being in thrall of Jupiter. If only it were merely the yips."
2. "Have you ever used a floral-based bath and shower gel along with a talky deodorant you mistakenly thought was balanced for normal sweat? Mulligan, you think?"
3. "I'm sorry. Past mistakes have caught up and become present agonies. Man, I gotta cut out the tomato butterscotch custard pie from the training table."
4. "I regret that, in my youth, I spent more time on the teeter-totter than on my swing."

Once schluff-putting has a starring role in your shot-making repertoire, you'll be able to score where it counts—in the golf world of commerce.

Psych 101

Schluffing can be thought of as a game plan on a dimmer switch: the raising or lowering of the game glow is dependent on the accurate reading of the subject at hand. How do you accurately analyze what makes someone tick and talk, and what's the best way to react once you've sorted it out? It's a tricky business, but the following three case studies should help.

CASE STUDY NO. 1: DIE HARDER

The behavior: Before playing, the subject meticulously lines up his clubs against a bench. This step is followed by the careful placement, in a particular order, of the clubs into his golf bag. In passing, you accidentally clip the first club with your toe. A domino effect ensues. He picks up a nine-iron and takes a swat at your coconut. His intention, he claims, is to improve your vision.

Play prepared

Why they do what they do:
(*a*) He's an obsessive-compulsive

personality (in layman's terms: a prune-challenged schnook);
(*b*) as a boy, when riled, he'd take up his ball and bat and beat his
buddies home.

Your reaction: (*a*) Inform him that, for bludgeoning, it's preferable
to use a mashie in those crucial few moments before regaining your
wits; (*b*) duck.

Your strategy—the dos and don'ts: (*a*) Do remember to wear
baseball catcher gear next time out; (*b*) don't speculate aloud as
to whether or not he's some crazed loner; (*c*) do schluff, but let
him know your caliber of play is in the .44 Magnum range;
(*d*) don't ask, by way of an icebreaker, which he thought was
funnier—*Caddyshack* or *Die Hard III*.

CASE STUDY NO. 2: HIDDEN TIGER, LEAPING GITTER

The behavior: The subject is a scratch player, but you are a hidden
Tiger. No matter how hard you try to mask your game, it's obvious
that you are that much better. The subject manages to smile peace-
fully through the first couple of holes—an unexcitable man, it
appears, enjoying a tight game. But when he finds himself down
four after the third, he explodes, springing forth and seizing you by
the arm in a vice-like grip that could body pierce Superman. He
shoots you a look—he knows where you live, so watch it, chump.

Why they do what they do: (*a*) He's a passive-aggressive personality
(in layman's terms: hidden dragon, leaping gitter; (*b*) as a baby, he
was wet-nursed by a wolverine.

Your reaction: (*a*) draw a chalk line for your murdered arm on the
green; (*b*) scream.

Your strategy—the dos and don'ts: (*a*) Do under-club schluff for offense, but over-club swings for defense; (*b*) don't attempt to enforce a "no horseplay" rule without first calling for backup; (*c*) do bring in clergy to caddy; (*d*) don't try to make an example of him by attempting to hang him *as* an effigy.

CASE STUDY NO. 3: THE BASKET CASE

The behavior: You've arranged the game and the tee time. You arrive in plenty of time, but the subject is late, cutting it very close. She finally arrives in a golf cart encased in a universal enclosure. The marine grade vinyl is smoked. It doesn't stop there—she insists on playing the entire round from the confines of the cart.

Why they do what they do: (*a*) The subject suffers from aerophobia (the fear of drafts) and agoraphobia (the fear of being in open and public places); (*b*) on a dark and stormy night, the infant subject was left as a foundling in a hamper at a mansion door—a trauma which left her, evidently, a basket case.

Your reaction: (*a*) "What the...?"; (*b*) ask if you should get a tea party set and join her for afternoon num-nums.

Your strategy—the dos and don'ts: (*a*) Do adhere to the spirit of schluffing by

"What the...?"

kicking your divots out of her wheel path; (*b*) don't insist that she *will* play outside the golf cart, even if it takes yards of bubble wrap; (*c*) do offer to play a round of drive-through mini-golf (a straight face is imperative); (*d*) don't poke your head in and ask if she, too, smells smoke.

Show Me the Money

Beyond personality analysis, business golf tactics can be made foolproof through a knowledge of the subject's corporate standing. Where *he* stands indicates where *you* ought to stand. The accompanying charts illustrate how awareness of corporate earnings can offer valuable hints regarding the appropriate game plan. Chart No. 1 (see pg. 66) analyzes corporate earnings and indicates the corresponding and correct level of schluffing. Chart No. 2 (see pg. 67) takes a different approach. Here, you'll see the relationship between misinformed course deportment and sound game plan preparation.

If, due to extenuating circumstances, you are unable to adequately research your subject's background, there are other ways to proceed. Consider the icebreaker story, attire and transportation.

Once upon a Time...
One of the greatest methods of raising your success potential comes via the golf story. It can be fun, it *must* be entertaining and it can let you icebreak without resorting to inane small talk. What follows is a fill-in-the-blanks form for a great golf story or anecdote.

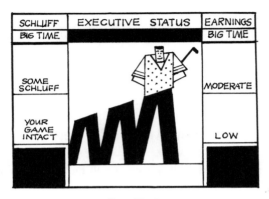

Chart No. 1

THE _____ OF _____: A FILL-IN-THE-BLANKS STORY

It was at _____ _____ _____. A _____ curled _____ behind and I _____ but it _____ me. Man, it had to be the _____ gosh darn _____ shank ever seen. What could _____ do? We decided to _____ and _____. So _____ whipped out his _____. Well, you imagine the _____. Unfazed, I _____ and rushed pell-mell _____ and using a _____-holed it. Several strokes later, I _____ under a stand of _____, shaking _____. It was not my best _____ _____ and from there I numbly proceeded to _____. Meanwhile, to everyone's surprise, _____ still managed to _____ when _____'s jaw clamped down on his _____. _____ marked it a _____. From then on, _____, but the unexpectedly corrosive foam _____ and _____. Frustration obviously brought out the _____ in _____. Where male vanity is _____, can _____ and oxygen facials be far behind, _____ wondered? Reality finally _____. We

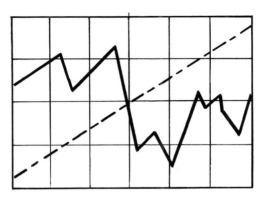

Chart No. 2

learned that less is definitely more. But give us the _____ and the _____ and the _____ and the _____ before unveiling a _____. In the bar afterwards, _____ gave _____ and_____ some fabulous advice: make sure you get dressed before going outside.

Effective as this form is, it should be used with restraint. Expanding the story to seventy-two holes is not generally recommended. If you get heckled at the most exciting bit, you might want to reconsider your approach. Ditto if sectarian violence breaks out during the sand blast scene. If your listener is calmly stuffing grass clippings into his ears or if you're asked to please switch to English, we'd suggest calling the whole thing off. Remember, a bad story can result in a done-in deal.

Dress for Success

While the icebreaker story is a key element of any successful business deal, it's only one piece of the puzzle. It's worth remembering that you'll likely be teeing off with the top dog (underlings are rarely sent out to enjoy warm, sunny days on the green). Discretion being the better part of armor, a proper dress code is a must. Here are some dos and don'ts:

- Do buy and wear conservative toggery. Tiger Woods did not become a $100,000,000 sports fashion plate by schlepping around in leisure wear knockoffs from the Liberace Museum.
- Don't purchase any golf wear with coupons (and avoid Dollar Daze sales like the plague).
- Do resist the temptation to dress in lawn furniture colors; and just say no to mixing plaids with reptile-skin prints.
- Do dress as if going to a funeral, and not to a tot's birthday party to make balloon animals.

Baby, You Can Drive My Cart

If you are what you eat, as the old maxim goes, then you might also drive what you drive. With the parking lot packed with BMWs, Mercedes and Jags, a golf cart choice can make or break opportunities. Here is some cautionary advice.

- Thumbs down, way down, on the ersatz jitney or rickshaw models.

- Pass by quickly, eyes forward, all vehicles with stylized flames emerging from the wheel wells.
- A golf cart sporting a plastic Rolls Royce grill won't fool anyone.
- Never take a chance on golf carts modified into angular caricatures of Bob Hope.

There's much at stake playing golf corporate style, and it's only after you succeed in your intentions that all the planning you do works to a tee. This, after all, is the puff that dealmaker dreams are made of.

4

Let the Games Begin

Fun, fun, fun till the caddy takes
our tee time away

Here's what we know so far. In this modern day and age—the Tiger Era, if you will—people seem to golf for one of a few reasons. They're either *in* the business (like Tiger, the CEO of the PGA and that world-famous course architect) or they're *doing* business (like your boss, your doctor and your accountant). So, whatever happened to fun? To golf for golf's sake?

What is fun? Dr. Samuel Johnson defined it as "sport; high merriment; frolicsome delight." Anon weighed in with "joy unrefined." In today's terms, though, fun is often a major cause for concern. We worry about whether we're having fun. We worry that others are having more than their fair share of fun and that there may not be enough fun to go around. (Some of us suspect hoarding: where there's a lot of laughter, there must be a lot of fun.) What's going on here? Is it possible that we're too serious about our fun?

A look at the golf course confirms this diagnosis. On any given afternoon, scattered amongst the doctors, lawyers and hockey players, a sharp eye can spot two distinct types of fun seekers: the Funatics and the Funsters. Funatics take their golf—and just about everything else they do—seriously. The Funsters? Well, the Funsters couldn't define "serious" if their collective lives depended on it.

Serious Fun

Who are the Funatics? You know the type. Their goal (nothing is done simply for a laugh) is to transform themselves into Tigers. They're the ones who never draw 9 PM tee off times; whose friends don't call them Bugsy, Harvey or Roger; and who are never, ever told that the only pro-am they'll make is the Ice-T Open.

Spot the Funster

For the Funatic, fun carries a lot of weight—weight one must work to overcome. (Note the conjunction of the words "fun," "weight" and "work": common usage in the Funatic lexicon.) The Funatic mind-set states that golf is a weighty game that must be worked at to be enjoyed.

Working at golf is by no means easy. As a rule, Funatics would prefer those not as serious about the game to practice their idea of fun elsewhere—preferably out of sight and out of mind. If asked to describe the Funatic approach to golf, most would reply along the following lines.

THE FUNATIC'S APPROACH TO GOLF

1. I am determined to have fun improving my swing.
2. I have to buckle down to correct my chip shot.
3. I mean business when it comes to lowering my handicap.
4. I took up golf in earnest to improve my quality of life.
5. I am seriously committed to having fun on the links.
6. If I put my shoulder to the wheel to improve my stance, the fun will be back in my backswing.
7. How can one have fun playing golf if one doesn't exert one's self?

The Funatic: serious fun

8. I'll have fun playing golf this year, come hell or high water.
9. At all costs, live or die, golf will be a pleasure.

For Funatics, golf is a labor of love (or maybe just a labor). Plunge a Funster into this sober world, and it's doubtful he'd survive the shock.

Dude, Did You Pack the Beer?

Funsters are exactly what their name implies—fun! They come in all shapes, sizes and dress codes. A tie-dyed T-shirt, ripped jeans and sandals might fit the bill. A baseball hat, worn backwards, is almost mandatory. Funsters have been known to try new and different golfing experiences: winter golf, Frisbee golf, extreme golf. Scorecards matter little to the Funster; beer matters a great deal. Unlike Funatics, Funsters would never dream of using the words "golf" and "work" in the same sentence.

THE FUNSTER'S APPROACH TO GOLF
1. A 9 PM tee off time works for me.
2. I'd classify my game style as *Field & Stream* meets *High Times*.
3. If I hit a birdie, will there be a taxidermist?
4. My only chance at a Grand Slam is a dark alley encounter with Arnold Schwarzenegger—but that's cool.
5. Do the greens come with a choice of dressing? If so, do you have Catalina?

6. I like those bright orange balls; they're easier to see in the deep rough.
7. Are cross-bunkers really angry or just a little miffed?
8. Tournament security? Does this fanny pack/first aid kit count?
9. We don't need no stinkin' Tiger.

Funsters are helpful folk. They're always ready and willing to share their strategies for fun on the links. Why not preplant a few mannequin arms reaching out of at least one bunker ("Beware Quicksand" signs are optional). Another favorite? Stash swordfishing rods and reels next to the water hazards.

Funsters also advocate maximizing the impact of tee shots.

The Funster's challenge

Consider playing them in this exact order: (*a*) miss ball completely; (*b*) stub ball three inches backwards; (*c*) clip ball three times in one brief series of jerky judderings; (*d*) assume a strange Tai Chi position you could later learn to enjoy; (*e*) shank ball off tee.

Should one of your foursome happen to find it not so amusing to have a golf ball pried from the back of his head, show him proof of an extra Y chromosome and blame it on that.

Like Oil and Water

It's clear that a chasm exists. While the Funsters are out having fun, the Funatics are working at it. For Funatics, the semblance of normal and innocent fun is an experience at once intense and life-changing. There are few Funsters around who, upon hearing this, can keep a straight face—another valid reason for the split between the two camps.

Are you a Funatic or a Funster? What about your friends? If you're still not sure where you sit on the fun scale, consider the following divergent approaches to some popular golf games.

BINGLE-BANGLE-BUNGLE
Funatic: Each hole is worth three points—one for being first on the green; one for being nearest the pin; and one for being first to sink a putt.
Funster: Bingle for the money, bangle for the show, bungle to get ready to go, cat, go.

The Funster plays Remorse

HIGH AND LOW
Funatic: Best ball wins.
Funster: Best Nerf ball wins.

THROW AWAY
Funatic: You may throw out your three worst holes.
Funster: If that's the game, a change of socks is needed all round.

REMORSE
Funatic: You can make your opponent replay any four shots.
Funster: Okay, any four shots may be replayed—but only with the help of a hypnotist who'll add to the fun by having the opponent cluck like a chicken.

ALIBI

Funatic: You may replay the number of shots equal to your handicap.

Funster: Um, I wasn't anywhere near those shots. I can get a guy to swear that I was draining a putt for an eagle across town. There was a tickertape parade. At least sixty people saw me waving from an open car. That's my alibi and I'm sticking to it.

A further example of the differences between Funatics and Funsters can be seen in the results of a simple test. Identical instructions for an admittedly unusual golf swing were given to each group. The resulting body language was carefully observed and annotated.

THE INSTRUCTIONS

1. Stand addressing the ball with your left hand gripping your golf club. Place your left hand in your right hand. Position your right hand so that it's touching your waist.

2. Tilt forward from the waist until your head feels heavy, causing some strain to your neck. Now, shift your weight to the ball of your left foot.

3. Tighten your grip on both your

The dandelion swing

waist and the golf club and pivot around on your right foot in a half turn.

4. Bring your left arm over your head until it's next to your left ear. Tip your forearm up a smidgen at the wrist.

5. Whirl three-quarters, raising your left hand in an arc-like gesture. Finally, dandelion swing at the ball.

BODY LANGUAGE: FUNATICS

1. Elephantine side to side swaying converts into rotational movements with spine as axis.

2. Arms fall in with rotation; hands are raised, clasped and lowered atop the head.

3. Right leg kicks out, scuffing ground with considerable intensity and vigor.

4. Torso tips forward from the waist; knees come together and bend.

5. Buttocks are thrust up and out.

6. Assumed position recalls that of a downhill skier.

7. Forward and back rocking ensues, accompanied by hissy-fit sounds.

BODY LANGUAGE: FUNSTERS

1. Body folds into a sitting position and rolls backwards onto ground.

2. Head is thrown back, mouth opens wide and legs begin pumping as if pedaling a phantom bicycle.

3. Arms shoot forward and hands play pat-a-cake on pumping

knees. A putt-putt sound not unlike a small boat is emitted, along with an unbridled series of snorts.

For those who need things clearly spelled out, here is an important table. Read it and learn.

FUNATIC VERSUS FUNSTER

Funatic	*Funster*
lockstep	knee jerk
nonexistence	coexistence
exercise = lesser evil	exercise = evil
buy expensive	buy priced to sell
dazzle	gloss
SUV	minivan
Bushmills	beer
golfer	guffer
Tom Hanks	Russell Crowe
Republican	why vote?
Tiger	Walrus
Wall Street	Mall Street
scratch player	duffer
navy blue	powder blue
classics	country classics
jogging	busing

It's also worth noting how each category defines the other. For Funsters, Funatics are self-destructive human beings with unpopular head shapes. The Funatics, for their part, believe the Funsters to be immature specimens with little or no human value. Enough said.

Home, Home on the Range

Despite their many differences, Funatics and Funsters both harbor a desire to play topline courses. Golf philosophy matters little when dreaming of Pebble Beach, Augusta, St. Andrews or Banff Springs. If and when the golden tee off time actually arrives, it's likely that the Funatics will be better prepared. What's a poor Funster to do? Short of packing up the beer and heading home, the only option might be a handy comeback.

HANDY FUNSTER COMEBACKS

1. It isn't *so* daunting once you know you can get a decent burial.
2. All the duck-hooking, grunching, toeing and slicing didn't have me worried—it was just friendly fire.
3. Something in the deep rough ate my putter.
4. The long irons we rented could double as pole vaults.
5. Arnold Palmer, Greg Norman and Tiger Woods played here? No wonder I shanked the place out—it's for golf nerds.
6. Hey, you'd stink too if you played the front nine the wrong way around.
7. We had to give up yelling "fore" in order to utter "uh-oh."
8. This place plays like a pastoral painting for a Road Runner cartoon.

9. Scorecards? We used jokers.
10. We think the guy who did the pin placements was a sozzled acupuncturist.

While Funsters clearly love the allure of a St. Andrews or a Pebble Beach, they may be better off at some of the sport's lesser venues. Star ratings for courses can be tip-offs as to whether or not fun is a key element. For edification, here is a Funster breakdown of just what those star ratings mean.

THE FUNSTER FIVE-STAR RATING SYSTEM

- *Five Stars*: (*a*) course trappings use live bait—you; (*b*) tee-side skull racks are thoughtfully provided for duffers who consistently hit their ball above center; (*c*) sound bite: "aiiieeee!"

The Five Star course: skull racks are thoughtfully provided

- *Four Stars*: (*a*) for duffers, "take-away" means swift removal by club marshals; (*b*) approach shots are better in the bar; (*c*) club tolerance for hackers? Think Texas wedgie; (*d*) sound bite: "aargh!"
- *Three Stars*: (*a*) the greatest feeling on this course is when you finally hole out; (*b*) course has attitude issues: big swing, under-clubbed; (*c*) sound bite: "p'tooie-e!"
- *Two Stars*: (*a*) punch bowl hollows contain real punch—spiked; (*b*) slicing, booking, topping, smothering, pulling, pushing, sky-ing, schluffing, shanking—nine fun shots on this lovely course; (*c*) sound bite: "ee-e-haw!"
- *One Star*: (*a*) hazards include cattle roundups and branding; (*b*) embarrassing (even for hackers) when you triple bogey trying to putt through a miniature Dutch windmill; (*c*) others in four-some wearing golf clothes so loud they could white-noise out a shuttle launch; (*d*) sound bite: "gack!"

Let's face it. As time wears on, not much about this particular arrangement is going to change. Funatics will continue to seriously have fun working at their games, and Funsters will remember that the games were invented so that the *players* could have fun *playing*. What a concept.

PART THREE

The Future

The future is an empty-headed ghost that promises all things and has nothing.

—Victor Hugo

5

Yesto Golf

Golf's destiny: past future perfect

What lies ahead for golf? If you and Chuckles Hugo are tight, the answer might be "nothing." But nothing is as certain as change—and, for golf, change is inevitable. The present slickly sweet concoction designed for conducting business brings to mind the state of pop music before punk. Punk "Sex Pistol–whipped" pop into renewed vitality only by stripping away the excess, crushing blandness and relying on the basics. This is a worthy paradigm for golf's future. Revisit days gone by and reapply the basics to give us a new game, reborn for the future. Call it Yesto Golf.

Required Course Work

What would the act of futurizing golf entail? The course itself would require significant changes. The architects—those nine-hatted wonders—offer a logical place to start. For some, Nature (in its natural state) would be as shocking as spontaneous combustion. It's not easy keeping greens. Anything that shows off their work—slick as an airbrushed photo—will be clutched to their bosoms with the passion of young lust. In order to dissuade designers from their cultish dependence on powerful chemicals, an intervention by deprogrammers from the Sierra Club is required. Consider the following three-step aversion therapy.

Confronting Nature

1. The architect is jostled into a seat that resembles a cross between a Barcalounger and an electric chair, strapped in tightly and restrained with heavy webbing. Eyes are propped open with caliper clamps (eyedropper spigots keep the eyes moistened) and joy-buzzers are affixed to palms.
2. A video montage of contrasts is shown: the manufacturing process of hot dogs and a block of tofu; an asphalt parking lot and a bucolic glade; Arnold Schwarzenegger and Woody Allen; Doctors Frankenstein and Dolittle. Musical accompaniment ranges from a death-metal version of Wagner's "Ride of the Valkyries" to an ambient-trance reworking of Beethoven's "Pastoral Symphony." Joy-buzzers zap the hands if any disdain for the latter side of the contrasting imagery is registered.

3. With their hands immersed in naturally composted soil, the architects are shown pictures of drooling bald guys (some formerly women) with orangutan bodies and heads like late fall turnips, putting on quasi-natural surfaces. This portion of the aversion therapy concludes with power hugs from actors costumed as Johnny Appleseed.

After completing the sessions, each architect will be given several written tests.

TRUE OR FALSE

Read the statement carefully and choose whether it is true (as in, correct) or false (as in, how wrong can one be?). Do not be afraid that your answers will reflect your problems, proclivities or personality. We're not concerned with what you *are*; only what you *do*.

1. A golf resort developer for whom you regularly work pays you a visit. You invite him to your new eco-conscious course. Upon arrival, your employer hops up and down with ecstatic, unbridled joy, trilling: "How utterly refreshing. Finally, golf meets *Lord of the Flies*! I like it. In fact, I luuuuv it! Blessings on you!"

    True   False

    (Circle one, and remember those joy-buzzers.)

2. Your employer comes to call. She asks you to show her the specs for her new resort development. When she sees your deep eco-golf plans, she says: "I understand. You know what's best.

As long as it makes Mother Nature happy, I'm happy, too.
Carry on with my good wishes."

> True   False

(Circle one, and remember: (*a*) your hand in the compost;
and (*b*) the guinea pig golfers that looked like inmates of a
fifteenth-century Italian madhouse.)

MULTIPLE CHOICE

Pick the answer that best completes the statement. Think first, and
remember the power hugs.

1. Now that you are a naturalist golf course architect, you
   should: (*a*) learn to live on $6,700 a year; (*b*) switch careers
   to something in hotel management or wall-to-wall carpet
   retailing; (*c*) feel proud; (*d*) change your name to Blotto and
   drop out, man.

2. Now that you're aware of chemical effects on the ecosystem,
   you should: (*a*) be suspicious of chrome-green grass; (*b*) know
   why crabgrass crabs; (*c*) know why you twitch like that.

3. Now that you're onside with Mother Nature, you should be
   able to tell what's eco-in from what's eco-out by: (*a*) the product's late-night infomercial, proclaiming to be golf's newest
   olfactory outlet sensation; (*b*) the product's claim to be decay-
   resistant and as nutritious as Styrofoam packing chips; (*c*) the
   arrival of a synthetic "sit-on-it" cactus, a gift from a spurned
   chemical supplier.

One Step Forward, Three Steps Back

While architects are off playing in the dirt, players will be
undergoing their own sort of intervention. Yesto Golf requires
the unlearning of contemporary techniques. This is not a process to
be undertaken lightly. Some are simply more comfortable with the
tried and true habits of modern-day golf. The following multiple
choice quiz will help determine whether you, as a player, have the
moxie to take this bumpy veer off the status quo.

GOLF AND YOU

1. I most enjoy driving: (*a*) in my gas-guzzling SUV; (*b*) a bargain;
   (*c*) on the links, on real grass.
2. Of the following, my favorite name is: (*a*) Hawg; (*b*)
   Terminator; (*c*) Nature Boy/Girl/Person.
3. Some of my closest friends are: (*a*) furriers; (*b*) extrusionists;
   (*c*) vegetarians.
4. All roads should lead to: (*a*) shopping malls; (*b*) motivational
   workshops; (*c*) the countryside.
5. My friends say I'm: (*a*) a gadget freak; (*b*) power-mad; (*c*) a tree
   hugger.
6. I would feel most secure knowing that I had: (*a*) unlimited
   credit at Prado; (*b*) natural body fluids; (*c*) clean air and a clean
   environment.
7. When annoyed at myself for taking a bogey, I: (*a*) drive dough-
   nuts with the golf cart all around the green; (*b*) sulk; (*c*) whistle
   a happy tune.

8. If I had to describe myself in just one word, it would be:
   (*a*) intense; (*b*) driven; (*c*) empathetic.

If you chose mostly A's, stick with what you know. A preponderance of B's suggests you're on the cusp. If C is the letter of the day, you're ready, willing and able to change. Go forth and Yesto.

For those with an aye to the future, there are really only two golf shots to unlearn: the drive (and its first cousin, the chip) and the putt. To begin, you'll have to let go of the disdain you may feel for the unorthodox duffer style of play. For some, this matches par with the warm feelings Bill Gates has for competing operating systems. When it comes to equipment, you'll also have to forget those clubs with the new-fangled stealth guidance systems.

Unlearning technique isn't about lowering expectations, moral collapse or even social death. (Okay, maybe not social death, but it's fair to warn you that you could be downgraded by peers to a B-list rating of "critical.") It's not even about straightening the pretzel. What's the mission statement? Loosen the grim grip of formality. Unlearning takes the Royal and Ancient game and steers it in a somewhat different direction. Take your pre-shot preparation, for example. What follows is a step-by-step guide to keeping loose and unlearned.

- Tense up legs, buttocks and thighs, stomach, back, neck, shoulders, jaw, face and eye muscles. Hold each muscle briefly, thinking: "Let's mambo!"
- Complete this breathe-easy exercise: inhale and hold

breath while mentally working out the probability factor for correctly predicting 117 consecutive cases of twisted ankle. Exhale slowly, all the while repeating: "Easy... easy... back off, easy now.... My hands are lethal with a golf club. I am licensed for this."

"Let's mambo!"

- Stay focused on the ball. Look at the ball. Notice it *is* a ball—not a mountain to move, a wedge of Brie or an ink blot. Say to yourself, "Ball, ball, ball, baloney." Do this until you crack up, you silly duffer.

- Partake in a mental rehearsal. Close your eyes, and in your mind's Cineplex, conjure yourself nailing all upcoming shots. Visualize this in stately slow motion. Obviously, you can't anticipate everything, but you can rehearse the basic moves. (For example, mentally rehearse your chip shot as it passes through that patch of brambles, the water hazard, the sand trap, off your partner's clavicle, through the water hazard again, past a tangle of gorse, coldcocking a sheep grazing on the green, out of the bunker where it landed when kicked by an incensed shepherd, into the water hazard again (deeper this time), the provisional, the green and, finally, the twelve putts for par.)

- Undertake a body rehearsal. Shadow-box your moves, closing your eyes so you don't see the guys in white uniforms running your way. Open your eyes and repeat the exercise, once in slow motion (as you wrest yourself free of their nets) and once at normal speed (as you run from their clutches).

FURTHER TIPS FOR UNLEARNING

1. Trouble with a rigid stance? Loosen your cleats for sudden, uncontrolled turns.
2. Overlapping grip bothering you? Lose it. Try the baseball, fire pole or toilet plunger grips. The Freemasons did, and look where it got them.
3. Muscle-memory lapses should be taken as encouraging signs. Work it, baby.
4. Feeling less than tip-top? It's an attitude change you need. Gout's flow. Gout's in the zone.
5. A tee off swing *can* contain such moves as the Left-Handed Twist Around, the Clumsy Carp Stumble, the Grab-Foot Jackknife and the Ignoble Three Bounce Fall-Down. Don't sweat it. Think of "what's wrong?" as a rhetorical question—in which case you'd be right.
6. Have trouble with a ball in a fried-egg lie? Don't get frustrated worrying about how much sand to take blasting it out. Sneak up on the ball. Jump quickly in front of it,

Show it your niblick!

surprising it, and show it your niblick! This should startle the ball out of its wretched lie, allowing you to whack the dimples out of it.

The final word? Rejoice in your deficiencies. If your swing looks like Houdini attempting to escape from an upside-down straitjacket, it's yips, yips, hooray! What you're doing wrong is right.

Bending the Rules

Golf is fairly unique in the sporting world: it's one of the few games where the rules are enforced by the players themselves. The introduction of Yesto Golf will have some effect on rules devised specifically for the modern style of play. Today's rules are summarized in *Golf Lessons*—a National Golf Foundation publication. Here are ten examples, with feedback from Yesto Golf's newly formed Rules Committee (YGRC).

Rule No. 1: Until you have holed out on the green, you may not touch your ball except by striking it with the club.
YGRC feedback: We have a problem with this. The no-touching rule is applicable to conventional golf courses, not those that feature exposure to the elements and barren, rugged landscapes. We'll just have to see how this one plays out.

Rule No. 2: After teeing off, play is continued toward the green with the player farthest from the flag hitting first. This order continues until all balls are in the hole.

YGRC feedback: As our course will lean toward the extreme as far as surface characteristics go, playing order must be flexible to accommodate action in riptide water hazards or mudslide bunkers.

Rule No. 3: If, at any time other than tee off, your ball moves after you have addressed it, add one penalty stroke to your score.

YGRC feedback: We consider this to be a form of balk. We reserve the right, under extreme climatic conditions, to waive the balk rule—unless a sledgehammer and nails are on hand to secure the tee to the ground and the ball to the tee.

Rule No. 4: Should your ball be lost in a water hazard or out of bounds, you must drop another ball as close as possible to the spot from which it was hit, counting that stroke and adding a penalty stroke to your score.

YGRC feedback: This is tricky. It's pertinent to remember that, although dropping a ball does guarantee a decent target line to the green, it does not guarantee that the dropper will eventually be marking his scorecard with souvenir pens. Our thought? Scuba.

Rule No. 5: When your ball lies in a hazard, you may not touch the ground, sand or water with the club until making the forward swing. Except for any movable, artificial obstructions that interfere

"You may not touch the ground."

(and may be removed), play the hazard as you find it in order to avoid the penalty of loss of two strokes.

YGRC feedback: We feel this rule veers dangerously toward metaphysics. It is unnatural for anyone, let alone a golfer, to *hover*. "You may not touch the ground" indeed. What were they thinking?

Rule No. 6: If your ball enters a water hazard, you may play it as is; or, under a penalty stroke, either (*i*) drop a ball behind the hazard in line with the hole and the point at which the ball last crossed the margin of the hazard, or (*ii*) drop a ball at the point from which your ball was originally hit.

YGRC feedback: Parts (*i*) and (*ii*) will not apply to our game as we allow use of such equipment as snorkels, goggles and easy-to-use, splatter-proof jiggers.

Rule No. 7: You may lift your ball from a man-made obstruction which interferes with your swing or stance (water pipe, protective screen, sprinkler), but not from an out-of-bounds stake or fence. *YGRC feedback*: As our mandate includes eco-awareness, we'd like to add the following to the list of man-made obstructions: radiation shields, beached tankers and abundant unidentifiable odors.

Rule No. 8: When your ball is on the putting green, if it lies in casual water, ground under repair or a hole made by a burrowing animal—or if such conditions intervene with the ball and hole—you may lift the ball and place it, without penalty, in the nearest position to where it lay, which affords maximum relief from these conditions without being nearer the hole. *YGRC feedback*: A tad wimpish here. Compliance would only be granted—and we emphasize *only*—if the conventional player is required to wear a paper hat marked "Trainee." We play 'em as is.

Rule No. 9: On the putting green, you may not touch the line of your putt except to (*i*) repair ball marks, (*ii*) remove loose impediments and/or (*iii*) clean your ball. Nor can you test the surface of the putting green by rolling a ball or scraping the surface. Penalty: two strokes. *YGRC feedback*: The stringency here is too overbearing. We like to help our players achieve a winning edge. Yesto Golf allows the use of a hoe.

Rule No. 10: Should your ball land on the wrong putting green, you may lift and drop it off the green (without penalty) within two club lengths of the nearest point that provides relief (but is no nearer to the hole you are playing).

YGRC feedback: Did the Rules Committee ever consider that the player might be engaged in several concurrent games? We find the assumption of lack of competence vaguely offensive. Perhaps it's time to give concurrency proper recognition.

Has it truly come to this? Don't panic—conventional golf hasn't reached that dreaded "or else" situation. Yet. But there's a lacuna to consider. Many of us believe that people are at their best as a *part* of Nature, not as its foe or conqueror. Following this logic, one might conclude that golf, closer to nature, could ascend to a level of nail-biting action unseen since goldfish were taught to fetch. Golf's future? Past future perfect—a place even tigers would fear to tread.